A
BOOK
OF
IRISH
AMERICAN
BLESSINGS
&PRAYERS

ANDREW M. GREELEY

FOR DAN HERR
WHOSE IDEA IT WAS

ISBN O-88347-269-4

CONTENTS

PRAYERS....

INTRODUCTION

Many years ago I began to bring a small collection of Irish blessings, mostly gathered from St. Patrick's Day cards, to St. Odilia's Church in Tucson where I was then doing weekend work. After I had exhausted the collection I returned to the usual blessing at the end of Mass. The people protested. Were there not more Irish blessings?

I began to search. All I could find was a collection of Irish curses— and wonderfully dreadful curses they were too! So I decided that I must try my hand at writing Irish-American, if not Irish, Blessings. Through the years at St. Odilia's and Our Mother of Sorrows in Tucson, at St. Mary of the Woods in Chicago, and on the dune at Grand Beach, Michigan on summer Saturdays, this collection grew. I offer them in print for all those who have asked whether they could find them somewhere and for those priests who have wondered whether I mind an occasional "borrowing." I don't mind at all. I'm flattered that anyone would want to use them.

A book reviewer (may their tribe decrease) remarked of a book in which some few of these previously appeared that I am not Seamus Heaney. Darn right! Neither am I James Joyce, William Butler Yeats, John M. Synge, G.K. Chesterton, or Graham Greene. So what? Why need I be to

make up my own blessings? Why need anyone be to make up their own blessings? If a priest reads this book and says, "I can do better than that!" more power to him. We need more blessings rather than less.

The prayers in the second half of the book were written after I had plowed through several collections of prayers, most of which seemed heavy, pompous and dull, and which, I suspect, would bore God should She be capable of that reaction. My prayers are mostly personal, one written for each day. I tried to pray in harmony with what I take to be the spirit of the Roman Liturgy which at its best is brisk, sober, and business-like.

The oldest prayers of the Roman Liturgy usually manage in two or three sentences (and sometimes one) to praise God, ask for His blessing and then to get on with the work at hand (amen). Why waste our time and God's with any more verbiage? This dignified alacrity is profoundly offensive to many contemporary liturgists who seem to think that the longer and more convoluted a prayer is, the better it is — as if God needed elaborate and detailed instructions from us to know what our needs are.

Like the blessings, the prayers are offered for those who may want to use them and as a spur to those who know they can do better.

AG
Chicago
April 1991

BLESSINGS

A BLESSING FOR FIFTY YEARS

May Brigid and Patrick bring joy to your heart
And the singing and dancing on this golden night
May you and all your true loves never part
And your path ahead be always bright
For now wisdom and grace and fun only start
And hope reaches forth to the coming of light
May you protect others from the scary dark
And see God's endless love make all things right

And May God bless you and grant you fifty more,
Father, Son and Holy Spirit

A BLESSING FOR A FESTIVAL

May Brigid shine her light on this fest
May Brendan see the voyage be blest
May Colum preside over song and jest
And Patrick guard each and every guest

May Herself grant that what is to come is best
Lady Wisdom hold the Durkins at her breast
May She and Jesus always be welcome guests
And ask with us what will they think of next

May they enjoy the peace of empty nest
And find hope in each surmounted test
May there be too much fun to need to rest
And may we all be asked to the next big fest

And may God bless all
Through the day and night
Until the morning sun
Father, Son and Holy Spirit

A WEDDING BLESSING

May Jesus and Mary guide you on your way
Through all of life's stops and starts
May the promise of this wedding day
Be kept alive in both your hearts

May the rhythms of daily life
Give new strength to your love and faith
May you triumph over foolish strife
And come home together sound and safe

May troubles give you in their turn
A challenge to begin again
May you with hope and joy thus learn
Surely that love need never end

May the God of passionate love bless you,
Father, Son and Holy Spirit

A BLESSING FOR JIMMY

Welcome to our wide wild world, wonder child,
And the waters that work it wilder still,
To a life yoked to the One sweet and mild
Who turned death to life on Golgotha hill

May his clear light lead you through gloom and dark
And his white robe promise both peace and fun
May holy oils your flesh for Eucharist mark
And may Mary guard you till home you come

May God Bless you
The Father who made it all
The Son who walked among us
The Spirit who lingers still

A BLESSING FOR A JUNE WEDDING

May God skim waves with you in years ahead
And charge with you against offensive lines
May you be healthy and happy and ever well fed
And watch TV at all appropriate times

May Mother Mary keep you close in love
So you love each other as her Son loves you
Till your lives continue in heaven above
And in eternity you're to each other true

May you welcome your guests with cheerful glee
And sing and tell stories with them all night long
May in one another you the Lord Jesus see
So that where you are he also belongs

May the God of love keep you always close,
Father, Son and Holy Ghost

A BLESSING FOR CHALLENGE

May the morning sun stir you out of bed
May the winter winds move you on the road
May the rains of March renew your strength
May the flowers of spring captivate your sight
May summer heat inflame your zeal
May autumn color stimulate your dreams
May the silver moon make you wiser yet
May you never be with yourself content
May Jesus and Mary keep you young
Full of life and laughter and love

And may the God of challenge and adventure
Bless you and keep you always
Father, Son and Holy Spirit

A BLESSING FOR VOCATION

May you hear the voice of God
In the raging storm
In the quiet breeze
In the city tumult
In the desert silence
In the loving whisper
In the angry cry
In classic harmony
In hard rock beat
In a modest hymn
In a roaring crowd
May you never miss the words
"I have fallen in love with thee
Oh my beloved, come follow me"

And may the God of invitations
And surprises and mysteries
Bless you and guide you always
Father, Son and Holy Spirit

A BLESSING AGAINST BAD THINGS

May Jesus and Mary
Protect you from
Falling stars
Crowded bars
Hateful words
Tiresome nerds
Hairpin turns
Dying ferns
Wind shear twist
Sunburn risk
Plunging stocks
Broken locks
Bears defeats
Muddy cleats
Russian flus
Winter blues
Ice cold feet
Love's retreat
Noisy teens
Worn out springs
Early burnout
Unfriendly clout
Traffic jams
The L.A. Rams

Bitter moods
Too rich food
Too much drink
Leaky sinks
Wind chill sting
And every other
Evil thing

And God cherish you
In the palm of her hand
And Bless you now and always,
Father, Son and Holy Spirit

A BLESSING FOR VALENTINE'S DAY

May your love be blessed by Valentine
And renewed by the God who loves us all
May sweet nothings your lover bind
And dark chocolate early love recall

May valentine lace revive the past
And your own romance, once more on fire,
In its passion experienced again at last
Reveal God present in your ardent desire

And may the God who created
Out of passionate love
Rekindle all your loves
So that you may know God better,
Father, Son and Holy Spirit

A BLESSING
FOR TRANSFIGURATION SUNDAY

May you see God

In the ice cream cloud
In the wild flower bloom
In the rose light at sunset
In the lover's tender eye

May you hear God

In the fall of rain drops
In the blowing wind
In the singing bird
In the child's gentle cry

May God touch you

In the friendly hand
In new washed linen
In the mesquite bark
In the lover's kiss

May you smell God

In the rosemary bush

In the orange blossom
In the lover's scent
In the rain swept sky

May you taste God
In dark chocolate
In raisin buns
In caring lips
And in cherry pie

And may God who lurks everywhere in love

Bless you, Father, Son, and Holy Spirit

A BLESSING FOR CHRISTMASTIME

May your eyes be alert for the sight of his face
And your ears ready for the sound of his voice
May your feet catch fire to run in his race
The song on your lips tell all the world "rejoice"

And may you clap and leap and shout and dance
Knowing that the Lord has come to set you free
And run down the road, a person entranced,
After the one who said come follow me

May God bless you
The Father who made you free
The Son who freed you once again
And the Spirit who keeps you forever free

A BLESSING FOR THE NEW YEAR

May you find truth in the year's smallest grace
And hope in the year's heaviest cross
May a pillar of light before your face
Drive off the darkness so you're never lost

May your journey be safe wherever you go
And the angels protect you from hassle and fuss
May you learn to walk a little bit slow
And to grow each day in hope and trust

And may the God of new beginnings
Grant you a New Year of love and peace
Father, Son and Holy Spirit

A BLESSING FOR GENEROSITY

May you be with goodness profligate
As winter is with flakes of snow
As fall with leaves of red and gold
To all, if early come, or late
And your friends' needs anticipate

When sagging spirits bring them low
May you warm them with your loving glow
As winter sun bathes a frozen lake
And may you be blessed
By the Father of profligate creation
The Son of superabundant wisdom
And the Spirit of exuberant love

A BLESSING FOR THE PRESENT MOMENT

May you treasure wisely this jeweled, gilded time
And cherish each day as an extra grace
Whose heedless loss would be a tragic crime
In today's tasks may you find God's tender face
May you know that to miss love's smallest chance
Is a lost opportunity, a senseless waste
May you see need in every anxious glance
May you sort out of the dull and commonplace
An invitation to God's merry, manic dance
And May the Lord of the Dance bless you
As He invites you to the dance of the hallowed
present
Father, Son and Holy Spirit

A BLESSING AGAINST PRIDE

May you ever know who you really are
An unimportant bit of cosmic dust
Yet more deeply loved than the brightest star
Tho you must give to others total trust

May you know how empty is the lonely self
And how full the open and fragile heart
May you be quick and brave to ask for help
Since without it your journey cannot start

And may the God who did not hesitate
To ask for your help and love bless you
Father, Son and Holy Spirit

A BLESSING FROM FEBRUARY SAINTS

May good St. Brigid keep you warm till spring
And fill your head with poetry and song
May your true heart with the help of Valentine
Love you deeply this month and all year long
May Blaise protect you from the common cold
And sore throat, hacking cough and snuffy nose
May Mother Mary's candles light your road
And at the end of the day bring sweet repose
And may God, who tells the stories of his love,
Through the saints, who love us too, bless you
Father, Son and Holy Spirit

A BLESSING FOR FRIENDS

May your parades be drenched by the cheerful sun
May your loves be smiled on by the friendly moon
May Jesus wait for you when life is done
And may Mary grant that it not be soon
May the wind brush softly against your face
May the daisies and daffodils line your way
May you be bathed by God's bounteous grace
And enjoy all the gifts for which you pray
And may you be blessed by the God
Who calls us all friends
Father, Son and Holy Spirit

A BLESSING FOR ASH WEDNESDAY

May the Lenten fast quicken your pace
And your spirit find wings to burst the sky
As you seek for the love in God's gentle face
Against the day when sadly you must die

May you not forget that you come from dust
And someday back to dust you must revert
Tho the day after that, without any fuss,
You'll have new life again, death being birth

May the Lord of Easter guide your Lenten pilgrimage
And, when it's time, bring you safely home
The Father, the Son and the Holy Spirit

A BLESSING FOR CONFIDENCE

May your hand be steady like a canyon rim
And your eye as clear as the desert sky
May your wit and wisdom never turn dim
And your wildest dreams, may they never die
May your laugh be strong when the world seems grim
May fretful, anxious tears all quickly dry
May Jesus watch over you with gentle cherubim
And Mary look down on you with loving eye
And may God bless you and increase your hope,
Father, Son and Holy Ghost

A BLESSING FOR MARCH'S SAINTS

May you dance a reel for St. Paddy's sake
And toast the many united in one
May St. Joseph guard you as soon as you wake
And safely lead you home when day is done
From Aquinas may you learn wisdom and truth
And from Gregory tradition's faithful way
May Casimir teach you courage and hope
And Gabriel surprise you each new day
Father, Son and Holy Spirit

A BLESSING FOR THE INCREASE OF LOVE

May the Spirit's warmth renew the love of your life
May God's strength help you to be brave
In tenderness, now weak in petty strife
May God's wisdom your sensitivity save
When frustration and discontent are rife
So that gently passion's bond be remade
May your delicacy be keen as a knife
And your gentle persistence never fade
Till love's old romance is at last remade
And may the God of Love bless you and
Bind you together as He binds the universe
With the attraction of gravity's power
Father, Son and Holy Spirit

A BLESSING FOR MARCH SEVENTEENTH

May it be a grand day for all of you
Be ye Irish or as Patrick as you'd like to be
May your jars be limited to just a few
May you revel in God's great diversity
In a land where Moslem, Protestant, Catholic, Jew
Enjoy a constitutional variety
Modestly raise a quiet cry and hue
To give thanks for peaceful ethnicity
And praise for pluralism's brightest jewel
Drink joyous toasts, in all sobriety
To the one from many neath red, white and blue

And may God bless you this glorious day
The Father who holds the world together
The Son who walked among us
And the Spirit who makes each of us unique

A BLESSING FOR TAKING LEAVE

May Brigid, Patrick and Colum smooth your trip
And all the other saints keep a watchful eye
So you lose not your balance and never slip
May Mary's gentle love be always nigh
May the Spirit's guidance you never lack
And on your journey let nothing go awry
May Brendan and Kiernan bring you safely back
But a moment after you've said good-bye
And may the God of journeys go with you on the way
And quickly bring you home again
Father, Son and Holy Spirit

A BLESSING FOR PASSIONTIDE

May the Sunday palms line your path
And the Seder bread unite your clan
May the Paschal Lamb set you free
And the candle fire renew our land

May this holy time heal all your pain
May you be close to God throughout the week
In the baptismal water may you live again
And find the Risen One for whom all seek

And may God bless you
The Father who created you
The Son who knows you
And the Spirit who enfolds you in love

A BLESSING FOR EASTER EVE

As our baptismal vows we all renew
May the Paschal candle expel the dark
While Christians joyously sing allelu
May the Easter water heal your heart

May you this holy time be born again
May you raise your head and clear your eyes
And when at last your life must end
Along with Jesus may you then arise

May the risen Savior flood you with life
And flame you with love
Together with the Father and the Holy Spirit

A BLESSING FOR A CRUCIFIX

May God bless this cross
And you who wear it
May you remember
That it stands for love
And generosity
And life that never ends
Father, Son and Holy Spirit

A BLESSING FOR EASTER TIME

May you have the strength to push away the sod
And to climb up out of the chilly tomb
May you respond to the trumpet call of God
And explode in life from death's clinging womb
May each day have its own wonder and rebirth
Its moulding of new life from unwilling clay
Its springing in surprise from reluctant earth
Its hint of victory on final judgment day
And may the God of daily resurrections bless you
Father, Son and Holy Spirit

A BLESSING AGAINST FEARS

May God protect you
From scary nights
From hasty fights
From too much food
From a somber mood
From ringing bells
From self-made hells
From sickish pains
From dishonest gains
From excessive needs
From tricky deeds
From foolish quarrels
From resting laurels
From silly fears
From idle tears
From forgotten lines
And from all bad times,
Father, Son and Holy Spirit

A BLESSING FOR MARY'S MONTH

May Mary's month explode with life
Flesh and fleece, fur and feather
Grass and green world, altogether
And make your world a paradise
May she turn you lush green with hope
When drops of blood and foam dapple
Bloom lights the orchard apple
Wrap you in her kaleidoscope
And madly paint you cardinal red
As azuring over greybell makes
Wood banks and brakes wash wet lakes
And with wonder dreams stuff your head
May she make you alive again
All things rising, all things sizing
Mary sees, sympathizing
Restores to birth what might have been

May the God of spring and new life bless you
And bring you life and hope and love
Father, Son and Holy Spirit

A BLESSING FOR MOTHER'S DAY

May Jesus and Mary bless and protect your home
And all who receive your tender care
May you be praised on this day of your own
May the sun shine brightly and the sky be fair

May you rejoice in your power to give life
And nourish with love those who clung to your breasts
May you protect them from anger and strife
And teach them that God's way is always the best

And may God who is mother as well as father
    bless you
The Father who gives life
The Son who nourishes
And the Spirit who cares

A BLESSING FOR FIRST COMMUNION

May Jesus and Mary be with you this day
As you offer your gifts of bread and wine
And may they take your hand and lead the way
As you come to the table for the very first time

May your life ne'er lack for its daily bread
Both something to drink and something to eat
With God's love may you be fully fed
And may you find its taste forever sweet

And may God in heaven love you and keep you
This day
And whenever you come to the Table
The Father, the Son and the Holy Spirit

A BLESSING FOR PENTECOST

May the warm promise of the rising sun
Flame all our hearts in Spirit's gracious fire
May God's invitation that we rise higher
Be confirmed in bright glory when day is done
May Pentecost faith burn like summer heat
That we speak with courage and prudent zeal
And the Gospel by word and deed reveal
Of God's love to kith and kin and all we meet

And May God bless you
The Father who sends
The Son who came
The Spirit who lingers with us

A BLESSING
FOR THE BEGINNING OF SUMMER

May the lake be smooth beneath your skis
And the winds blow wide your colored sails
May the sand be warm as you take your ease
And God's grace bathe you that never fails

May the sun shine bright on your joyous days
And the rain refresh you through peaceful nights
May summer show you God's wondrous ways
And prepare you for heaven's great delights

Till we meet there
May the God of summertime
Hold you in the palm of her hand
Father, Son and Holy Spirit

A BLESSING FOR GRADUATION DAY

May this day be totally cool
As you look forward to life's next test
And give you thanks to those who did their best
To teach you something here in school
May learning linger in your head
And perhaps a little wisdom too
Be confident in all you do
And don't be afraid, laugh instead
May you be wrapped in God's loving grace
As the moon in a misty cloud
May you hear God's voice, clear and loud
In pilgrimage to his dwelling place

And May God bless you
The Father who created you
The Son who teaches you
The Spirit who guides you through life

A BLESSING FOR STRENGTH

May God's strength for you be
As strong as the typhoon wind
As faithful as the daily tide
As sweet as music of the violin
As pervasive as the starry sky

May God's care for you be
As light as a singing thrush
As swift as a mountain stream
As gentle as a baby's touch
As alluring as a lover's gleam

And may God bless you
The Father of power and strength
The Son of wisdom and knowledge
The Spirit of loving care

A BLESSING
FOR A WEDDING ANNIVERSARY

May wild red roses line your path
And the rains of spring clean the air
May you heed the wisdom of your past
And serve each other with grateful care

May Mary be with you on your way
May your children return all your love
May you grow closer with each passing day
Till you go home to God in heaven above

May the God of love
Keep your love as warm as the summer sun
Father, Son and Holy Spirit

A BLESSING FOR THE FOURTH OF JULY

While the red flame of sunset warms each of you
And snow white clouds point to heaven's door
May you be wrapped in Mary's mantle blue
That your land be free forever more

May God grant you long years of life
And liberty to serve each other's need
May happiness chase all foolish strife
May you seek his peace in each word and deed
Father, Son and Holy Spirit

A BLESSING
FOR LITTLE CHILDREN AT NIGHT

Rest peaceful, small marvel, in your little bed
Be protected from dark terrors of the night
May God's grace linger on your splendid head
And keep you warm till the coming back of light

May Jesus and Mary watch you always
And keep you wise and healthy, safe and sound
Be well loved through your journey's nights and days
Till all of us in peace and joy abound

And may God bless you and keep you, wonderchild,
Always and forever and even after that
Father, Son and Holy Spirit

A BLESSING DURING A JULY HEAT SPELL

May soft nighttime breezes touch your face
And friendship's peace refresh your life
May you be cooled by God's loving grace
And avoid all ill-tempered strife
May you sing with the dancing rain
For heat and cold and all God's shows
Which make the seasons come again
And in a few months bring winter's snows
Father, Son and Holy Spirit

A BLESSING
FOR A YOUNG GIRL IN SUMMERTIME

May you swim in warm and gentle waves
Under clear skies that match your timeless eyes
May Jesus and Mary keep you sound and safe
And lead you to womanhood, healthy and wise
May the sand move softly beneath your feet
May the angels frolic when you play and sing
May the trees shade you from the summer heat
And may summer sweet surprises always bring

And May God bless you
The Father who created you
The Son who showed you how to live
And the Spirit who loves you

A BLESSING FOR GOD'S MERCY

May God's mercy wash you like an April rain
And as quicksilver mist dance before your eyes
As it waits in busy street and quiet lane

May mercy cover you like the morning sky
And tread lightly in silent time and empty space
And you be ready for God's BANG surprise

May you find that there is no godless place
May you welcome mercy in whatever guise
And may you never run from forgiving grace

And may the God of mercy bless you
Father, Son and Holy Spirit

A BLESSING FOR WONDER

Listen for cheerful birds at song
Revel in a friendly smile
Grasp the offered hand, warm and strong
With your best love be reconciled

Watch the clouds march across the sky
As you come from daily labor
Your heart open for surprise
To your home, that is, Mount Tabor

And may the God of surprises
Who filled the world with wonder
To reveal Himself
Bless you, Father, Son and Holy Spirit

A BLESSING FOR COMING HOME

May the door swing open with cheerful charm
And the old familiar mutt jump and bark
May everyone you love wait with welcome arms
And the light of friends chase away the dark
May Mary keep your home from all wicked harm
May you sing and dance and talk and play all night
May your grace and kindness all fear disarm
May you wait a day before your first good fight
May the God of homecomings welcome you home
Each day and at the end of all our days
And forevermore, Father, Son and Holy Spirit

A BLESSING BEFORE MEALS

May the Lord God be with us at this meal
And bless us and the food we're about to eat
May this table our love and friendship seal
As we give thanks for our bread and wine and meat
May we be gracious to those who come in need
And to the lonely ones we perhaps can heal
In those who want, the Lord's holy presence heed
And gratitude to our cook most profoundly feel
Father, Son and Holy Spirit

A BLESSING
FOR MARY'S DAY IN HARVEST

May your family never lack food to eat
May you feed the hungry before you dine
May your table be heaped high with tasty meat
At your feasts may you serve the best of wine

May Our Lady guard you from all God's foes
And may her loving care you never lack
If the front gates of heaven are firmly closed
May Mother Mary sneak you in the back

And may the God of the harvest and the vintage
The God of bread and wine
The God of food and drink
Bless you, Father, Son and Holy Spirit

A BLESSING FOR LABOR DAY

May your work bring order where there was chaos
Wisdom where there was ignorance
Brightness where there was obscurity
Purpose where there was confusion
Warmth where there was harshness
Laughter where there was pain
Challenge where there was boredom
And God's holy peace where there was hate
May you create in the name of the God who creates
Be wise in the name of God's revealing word
And loving in the cause of God's Spirit who serves

A BLESSING
FOR GOING BACK TO SCHOOL

May your unprepared answers be almost right
And all your teachers only be the best
May too much homework never spoil a night
And may you get at least a hundred in every test

May you study hard and learn a lot
Of reading and writing and God's love for us
No matter how deep the snow, forget you not
That soon it will be summertime again

And may Jesus who grew in wisdom and age
    and grace
Bless you together with the Father and the Holy Spirit

A BLESSING FOR THE SACRAMENT OF RECONCILIATION

May you have the clarity to face the facts
And wisdom to understand your grievous faults
May you find patience to start again from scratch
And faith that you are the earth's treasured salt

May you sorrow for the hope you have betrayed
And lament for every promise blighted
May you rejoice that guilt surely is allayed
By God's love thru which all wrongs are righted

And may God forgive your sins and renew your life
Father, Son and Holy Spirit

A BLESSING
FOR GOING AWAY TO COLLEGE

May the autumn leaves carpet beneath your feet
And the angels lead you through the class day maze
May your homecoming time be extra sweet
And your heart warm with Indian summer days
Like Jesus may you grow in wisdom, age and grace
May you learn to read and write and think and sing
May you swiftly run in learning's rapid race
And God's kind love to all your roommates bring

May God hold you in the palm of his hand
Until we meet again
And keep you safe and well
Father, Son and Holy Spirit

A BLESSING FOR THE DAY

May the God of the misty dawn waken you
May the God of the rising sun stir you up
May the God of morning sky send you on your way
May the God of noonday stillness renew your strength
May the God of afternoon bring you home
May the God of sunset delight your eye
May the God of twilight calm your nerves
And May the God of dusk bring you peace

And may God bless you
The Rising and the Setting Sun
The Alpha and the Omega
The Beginning and the End
Father, Son and Holy Spirit

A BLESSING FOR A SUNDAY IN OCTOBER

May your joy be as bright as October red
And your friends as strong as autumn gold
May Mary protect you from fear and dread
And Brigid warm you through winter cold
May you relax in Indian summer peace
And walk serenely in smoky evening light
May you know that God's love will never cease
And after winter comes spring delight

And May God bless you
The Father who creates the stars and the seasons
The Son who came with spring for everyone
And the Spirit who turns the world in love

A BLESSING FOR AN OCTOBER WEDDING

May leaves of autumn decorate your path
May mellow golden sunlight guide your way
May love and laughter overcome all wrath
And renew the joy of your wedding day
May October warmth turn away the cold
And Indian summer haze soothe life's pain
May God protect your romance from growing old
And, if it wilts, refresh your love again

And may God bless you and keep you always
The Father who creates love
The Son who renews it
And the Holy Spirit who guards us from the cold

A BLESSING FOR A ROSARY

May God bless these rosary beads
And you who with them devoutly prays
May He be kind to all your needs
On this and your remaining days
In glory, sorrow and every joy
May Mary be with you on the way
May no evil your peace destroy
And each month glow as bright as May
Father, Son and Holy Spirit

A BLESSING FOR A DANCING GOD

May the tunes of angels echo in your brain
May heaven's rhythms tap your twitching feet
May you sing along with Mary's sweet refrain
And may you sway to the Lord's demanding beat
Dance with all the lovers He has taught your song
And, sure, spin with Himself at every chance
Whenever He invites you all night long
Never say no to the Lord of the Dance
May the Lord of the Dance bless you and lead you in
The dance, Father, Son and Holy Spirit

A BLESSING AGAINST ENVY

May you celebrate your neighbor's happy days
May you always rejoice when a friend succeeds
And with a generous heart sing his praise
And know that God judges us not by others' deeds

May green-eyed envy be banished from your life
May you never demean another's work
May your soul be immune from its vicious strife
And your face be free of its nasty smirk

And may God bless you
The Father who gave you your talents
The Son who died because of envy
And the Spirit in whose way it stands

A BLESSING FOR THE NIGHT

May the God of heaven's vault bless you
May the God of shimmering moonlight love you
May the God of sparkling stars lead you
May the God of haunting songs cheer you

May the God of strange shadows calm your nerves
May the God of straight roads bring you home
May God be watching from a familiar window
And hand in hand with him may you wait for dawn

And may the God of day and night
Bless you, Father, Son and Holy Spirit

A BLESSING FOR THANKSGIVING

May your family gather in joyous peace
May the cranberry relish charm your taste
Enjoy your turkey in a happy feast
And finish off with pumpkin pie as grace

May you thank the Lord with all your strength
For food and drink and love and friends
For his goodness through life's long length
And his promise of a Eucharist that never ends

And may the Lord of the Eucharist bless you
Father, Son and Holy Spirit

A BLESSING FOR FAITH

May your faith be strong as a mountain wall
And subtle as the early morning mists
May you believe that God's power conquers all
And his love through trouble and pain persists

May your faith soar like a multicolored bird
And shine brighter than the blinding desert sun
Because you know your prayers are ever heard
And Jesus waits when the final day is done

And may God bless you,
The Father who rules the starry skies
The Son who rose from the dead
And the Spirit who comes in hope

A BLESSING FOR A WINTER WEDDING

As warm bread is sliced by a gleaming knife
May sunlight cut through the harsh winter cold
May God's love shine brightly in your common life
And may your own romance be never old
May hope increase with each lengthening day
And rout the ache of hurt and conflict's gloom
May loyal friends never be far away
With the promise that spring will surely bloom
May our good God of songs round the fireplace
Of love and laughter, of good wine and fun
Lurk always in your home's hidden space
And bind you in love when each day is done

And may God bless you and keep you close,
Father, Son and Holy Spirit

A BLESSING FOR HOPE

May your hope be as swift as a horse racing by
As deep as the bowels of earth
As high as the star-dense sky
As fresh as a baby's birth

May it be as strong as gravity's force
As resilient as a mother's love
As tenacious as a river's course
As timeless as the gentle Lord above
And may God bless you and renew your hope
Father, Son and Holy Spirit

A BLESSING
FOR THE SUNDAY BEFORE CHRISTMAS

May your warm heart make straight His path
May your generosity smooth His way
May they know He comes because you laugh
And see the Child in you on Christmas day
May you too be a light shining in the dark
A candle calling loved ones home
Inviting flavor in the pastry tart
A sky, clear and crisp, under heaven's dome
And may the God of Christmas bless you
The Father who made the world in love
The Son who came on Christmas night
And the Holy Spirit who calls us home

A BLESSING
FOR THE COMING OF SANTA CLAUS

May you ever reach for the highest star
And dream the most impossible dreams
Never be content with the way things are
But yearn to dance on heaven's scenes
Receive the smallest gift with holy awe
And make your own gifts David's key
Yourself for love act like merry Claus
By your own light shining at the tree
May the God of Little Children
Of St. Gabriel and St. Nicholas
Bless your Christmas dreams
Father, Son and Holy Spirit

A BLESSING FOR CHRISTMAS EVE

On this Holy Night may you be
As solid as the contented ox
As gentle as the placid lamb
As merry as the shepherd kids
As eager as the pilgrim kings
As bright as the angel songs
As strong as Joseph's smile
As bright as the new born babe
And as happy as Mother Mary
With Jesus in Her arms
And may Emmanuel, God with us,
Come to your own Bethlehem
This Holy Night
Father, Son and Holy Spirit

A BLESSING FOR CHRISTMAS

Each Christmas comes as a surprising gift
Like an infant's first tiny tottering step
Or a rediscovered lover's tender touch
And after a stormy night, soothing dawn
Snowflakes lightly dusting a frozen field
The smile of hope in a hurrying crowd
Pardon long delayed then quickly given
Candlelight which fractures the winter gloom

May delight lurk for you at every turn
Amid all the evergreen and mistletoe
And tissued heaps of tinsel ribboned gifts
May Christmas wonder renew your deepest loves
With whom go hand in hand to Bethlehem
To be surprised by the Mother and Her child

May God bless you
The Father, Son and Holy Spirit

A BLESSING FOR CHRISTMAS DAY

May you be heaped high with wondrous gifts
And trapped often neath the mistletoe
And loved by hearts light and swift
As gentle as newly fallen snow
May the Star shine brightly on your tree
And angels guarantee your fun
For with Jesus we are once more free
And our new life has just begun
May God Bless you
And all you love
On this Holy Day
Father, Son and Holy Spirit

A BLESSING FOR STEPHEN'S DAY

May the Prince of Peace bring you peace
May the Light of the world shine in your heart
May the Root of Jesse make you strong
May the Key of David open your love
May the Rising Sun light your path
May Adonai lead you home
May Emanuel be always with you
And may God lift your hope
This day after Christmas
Father, Son and Holy Spirit

A BLESSING FOR MARY'S DAY AT CHRISTMAS (JANUARY 1)

May the one who gave us Jesus child
And the whole world a life reborn
Mary, strong and meek, fierce and mild
Bless the new year that starts this morn
Protect us, guide us, heal our tears
Bring us love and hope and mighty faith
Exorcise all our foolish fears
And keep us warm with loving grace
May God bless you
The Father who made
The seconds and the years
The Son who lives in time
And the Spirit who leads the cosmic dance

A BLESSING FOR LITTLE CHRISTMAS

May you always follow your inviting star
Across the desert sands dull and dry
Away from home, whether near or far,
Watch not the bitter earth but the starry sky
May you delight in wonder unforeseen
New adventures only now begun
May your life never become dull routine
While you search for Mary and her Son
And may the God of adventure and pilgrimage
Bless you on your way
The Father who made the star
The Son for whom it shone
And the Spirit who calls us home

A BLESSING FOR CANA SUNDAY

May you never lack a glass of good red wine
And loyal friends to drink it with thru your life
May your love not weary with the drift of time
And the most lovely woman be your wife

When passion is frozen by winter cold
May there come to your house the Lord of the Dance
So that you show God's grace to all the world
With the great peat fire of your renewed romance

And may the God of Cana
The God of water made wine
The God of parties made fun
The God of love made new
Bless you, Father, Son and Holy Spirit

A BLESSING FOR WATER SKIERS

May mighty Michigan be smooth as glass
And your run untroubled by contentious wakes
May your fuel tank always be filled with gas
And your ski rope the brand that never breaks

May high as the sky be your dazzling spray
And the slalom course become a piece of cake
May you always be guarded on your spinning sway
By the same good God who walked Galilee's lake

And may God bless you
The Father who created from water
The Son who walked on water
And the Holy Spirit who hovers over it

A BLESSING FOR A SILVER ANNIVERSARY

May a silver moon reign over this harvest night
And glorious Irish dreams explode anew
May those glittering blue eyes dance with light
While argent stars whirl to the pipes with you

May your journey be at least twice as long
And your kids prevent you from growing old
May Jesus and Mary join in your song
And henceforth may every day be purest gold

And may the Lord of the Great Sacrament
Bless you, Father, Son and Holy Spirit

A BLESSING
FOR A GOLDEN WEDDING ANNIVERSARY

May your pilgrimage to the rainbow colored lands
Go joyous on a glowing yellow brick way
By a gentle sea, across the glittering sands
Wrapped in the friendly warmth of middle day
May you realize that God's golden light
Which oft urges you to quickly hasten on
And escape the frightening shades of night
Is not fading sunset but exploding dawn
And may God Bless you
The Father who created you
The Son who showed you God's goodness
And the Holy Spirit who
Binds you, like them, in love

A BLESSING
FOR THE FAMILY OF A DEAD INFANT

May our holy faith wipe away your tears
And God's love soon restore your smiles
May you heal one another's haunting fears
Because death triumphs for but a little while

May you bear the pain as long as it must last
Since thru our cross each must show love's worth
And when the long night of dour grief is past
Remember, in the sunrise, that death is birth

And may the God of the eternal day
Bring you hope and peace,
Father, Son and Holy Spirit

A BLESSING FOR A NEW BISHOP

May you grow richer in your people's love
And wiser in their candid honesty
May you listen like a prudent dove
May you be as solid as a redwood tree
And a pillar of light for troubled youth
To love God may you set your people free
May your work among us bear abundant fruit
May torrents of grace wash you from above
And always may you speak and hear the truth

And May God bless you
The Father with his strength
The Son with his wisdom
And the Holy Spirit with
Her discerning love

A BLESSING
FOR A HIGH SCHOOL ACTRESS

May you sing each note loud and clear
May your diction be articulate and precise
May you survive that curtain rising fear
And the audience think you're cool as ice

May you remember every single line
And your talents from God always cherish
May you sing in his honor all the time
And may the whole world become your parish

And may the God of Song and Dance bless you
The Father who started the dance
The Son who calls the tune
And the Spirit who plays the pipes

A BLESSING FOR A SILVER JUBILEE

As agile silver moonbeams dance upon the waves
May God's love and mercy circle you today
With living laughter that renews and saves
And bright hope to lead you further on your way

In your sermons may you celebrate his word
And for your people challenge and comfort be
A witness for a gentle and gracious Lord
At least until your diamond jubilee

And may God bless you
The Father to whom you offer
The Son for whom you stand
And the Spirit in whom you preach

A BLESSING FOR A GOLDEN JUBILEE

May you look back with confidence and pride
And forward with a twinkle in your eyes
May you enjoy the challenge of every ride
And await tomorrow with openness to surprise

May God's dazzling love dance before your face
When you offer his Eucharistic meal
May He envelop you in his loving grace
As He renews your ordination zeal

And May God Bless you
The Father whom we serve
The Son whom we follow
And the Spirit who protects on the way

A BLESSING
FOR A NEWLY BAPTIZED INFANT

May you be spirited by the water's flow
And dazzle all in your shining Easter dress
May your life reflect the Christ-candle glow
And the holy oil challenge you to your best

May you sleep peacefully in the Church's care
And awake with eager and laughing heart
Responding to God's offered love affair
Whatever the Lord wants you'll do your part

And the God who brought to life in an act of love
And offers you life as a revelation of his love
Bless you and protect you with that love
Father, Son and Holy Spirit

A BLESSING FOR A MEDAL

May this medal fix on your mind
The image of God who loves us all
Who is ever gentle and kind
And picks us up when we slip or fall
May He guard you from evil's traps
And watch over you day and night
That your faith may never collapse
As you walk always the path of light

May God bless this medal
Father, Son and Holy Spirit

A BLESSING FOR VISION

May you see as clearly as Mary on Christmas morning
As carefully as Joseph on the desert flight
As perceptively as John on the Jordan banks
As bravely as the twelve whom Jesus called
As wildly as the Palm Sunday throng
As sadly as the women neath the cross
As gratefully as the forgiven thief
And as joyously as Mary on Easter morn
And may the God of sight make us all to see
Father, Son and Holy Spirit

A BLESSING FOR A WEDDING IN MAY

May Jesus bless and bind your love today
May Mary keep your pledge alive and strong
May spring flowers bright always mark your way
And blue skies shelter a journey safe and long
May conflict never take your peace away
May good friends protect you from every wrong
May you answer always God's call to play
And your eyes sparkle with laughter, joy and song
And may the God who changed water into wine
Bless and protect your life together
Father, Son and Holy Spirit

A BLESSING FOR AN ENGAGEMENT

May Jesus and Mary make straight your road
May blue skies shine on all your parades
May your years stretch on to silver and gold
May your love be the sort that never fades

For every winter may there come a spring
For every hurt a quick and healing hand
For every doubt the hope that's in this ring
For every fear the promise in this magic band

May God bless you
The Father who created love
The Son who came in love
And the Spirit who keeps love alive

A BLESSING FOR ST. JOSEPH'S DAY

May St. Joseph protect you on your way
Through dark nights and humid days
Through thunderstorms and ruined parades

And may he win for you in loneliness and pain
The faith and hope to begin again
May he grant you strength when you are weary
Laughter when your times are sad
Vision when your eyes are bleary
And patience when your kids are bad
And as he brought Jesus and Mary
Home to Nazareth
May he bring you home finally
In peace and joy

And may God, like Joseph always faithful,
Bless you, Father, Son and Holy Spirit

A BLESSING FOR HOPE

May your hope be

As determined as the river racing by
As soft as the cry of the morning dove
As sweet and subtle as a lover's sigh
As glorious as reborn human love

As resolute as the sun rising each day
As certain as the return each year of spring
May it break through the darkling clouds
And confirm you against every evil thing

May Jesus and Mary and Patrick and Brigid
Strengthen your faith and hope and Love

And may God bless you, Father, Son and Holy Spirit

A BLESSING FOR THE NEARNESS OF GOD

May you be as close to God

As the sheep is to the shepherd
As the branch is to the vine
As the flower is to the stem
As the bride is to her groom

As the fish is to the water
As the bird is to the air
As the star is to the sky
As the heat is to the sun

As the plant to its seed
As the leaf to its branch
As the child to her mother
And as God is close to you

And may the God who loves you
Be always with you and bless you
Father, Son and Holy Spirit

A BLESSING FOR COMPUTER USERS

May Brigid and Gabriel
Keep your floppy disks unsmashed
And your printer feed unjammed
Your hard disk head uncrashed
And from confusing Rom and Ram

May they remind you
To back up all your text
What all your macros mean
And to rest your weary eyes
From the glaring amber screen

May they keep your
Backbone straight, your belly lean
And your dangerous temper mild
Your gentle smile serene
And your patience undefiled

And may God, for whom the world is a PC
Bless you, Father, Son and Holy Spirit

(Gabriel is the patron of those who work with electronic communications and Brigid the patron of poetry and story telling.)

A BLESSING FOR JOY

May Jesus and Mary and Patrick
Grant you happiness and joy
Festivity, celebration and also fun
Broad hints of glee without alloy
When at last our work is done

The joy of Easter morn
The joy of Christmas night
The joy of a new baby born
The joy of all delights

The joy of a graduation class
The joy of delicious food
The joy of a wedding mass
The joy of old love renewed

And may Jesus who came to bring us joy
Bless you always, together with
The Father and the Holy Spirit

A LITANY FOR OUR LADY

Mother of the budding earth, pray for us
Mother of the flourishing fields
Mother of the ample harvest
Mother of the family meal
Mother of the poor and sick
Mother of the lonely and forgotten
Mother of Jesus
Mother of all of us
Lady of the quiet days
Lady of the peaceful nights
Lady of song and dance
Lady of poem and story
Lady of burning love
Lady of broken heart
Lady of peace and freedom
Lady whom God desired
Lady of all of us
Queen of little children
Queen of troubled teens
Queen of husbands and wives
Queen of priests and nuns
Queen of all the world
Queen of peace
Pray for us

A BLESSING
FOR GOOD SHEPHERD SUNDAY

May the Good Shepherd protect you in

Ups and downs
Ins and outs
Bounds and rebounds
High and lows
Comings and goings
Heat and cold
Darkness and light
Joy and sorrow
Good times and bad times
Day times and night times
Short times and long times
Old times and new times

May He be with you

At home and abroad
On the road and at rest
In storm and flood
In drought and desert
In peace and conflict
In doubt and assurance
In sickness and health

In pain and triumph

May the Good Shepherd walk with you always
Until it is time to return home

And may God bless you, Father, Son and Holy Spirit

A BLESSING FOR A WORK OF ART

May this carefully crafted image,
A story of God's gracious love
Lurking softly in our lonely world,
Lift your mind to heaven above

May Jesus and Mary bless it and you,
This sacred and holy sign,
And your imagination sanctify
And your every place and time

May Jesus who left his image
On Veronica's towel
Bless this image
Together with the Father
and the Holy Spirit

A BLESSING FOR AN AIRPLANE

May Colum and Michael bless this plane
May those who fly it never fear
Fog and lightning and heavy rain
In their sky may the good God be near

In takeoff may it be safe and brisk
In landings always deft and light
May it fly through clouds with little risk
And may angels join it late at night

May Jesus who ascended into heaven
Bless this plane and crew
And all who fly through the sky
Together with the Father and the Holy Spirit

A BLESSING FOR A BOAT

May Nicholas and Brendan bless this craft
May angels dance above its deck
To ward off dangers fore and aft
From wind and wave and sunken wreck
All who sail it may they protect
And may all who cruise this mighty lake
Treat it always with wise respect
And no foolish risks ever take

May Jesus who preached from a boat
Bless and protect this boat
Together with the Father and the Holy Spirit

A BLESSING FOR AN AUTOMOBILE

May Christopher and Brendan bless this car
And all, young or old, who ride in it
May their trips be safe, near or far
And they never speed beyond the limit

May they drive with courtesy and care
And see God's face behind other wheels
May they never lack a handy spare
And for poor pedestrians compassion feel

May Jesus, himself a pedestrian, bless this auto
Together with the Father and the Holy Spirit

A BLESSING FOR AN UNBORN BABY

May Madonna and Child protect this babe
May the child be welcome, girl or boy,
And enter the world healthy and safe
And may mom and dad be filled with joy
In their child see a hint of immortality
And celebrate with laughter and mirth
That new life is the ultimate reality
For birth is death and death is birth

May Jesus who was once an unborn babe
Bless this mother and child
Together with the Father and the Holy Spirit

A BLESSING FOR A WEDDING

May Jesus and Mary be at your side
As close to you as your wedding rings
Where you are may they abide
And angels shade you neath their wings

May the quick, warm winds of spring
Sweep away all grimy clouds
Joy and happiness ever bring
And exorcise any deadly doubts

May your love be never ending
And may you one another guide
Onward from this happy wedding
And from each other never hide

Two lovers in whatever crowd,
To each other may you always cling
Of your hope and laughter proud
In good and bad and everything

May Jesus who came to Cana and
His mother who saved the party
Protect you always
And may He bless you together
With the Father and the Holy Spirit Spirit.

A BLESSING FOR A YOUNG MAN
IN SUMMERTIME

May Jesus and Mary protect you this summer from

Broken bones
Skinned knees
Throwing stones
And stinging bees

Sibling fights
Irate moms
Too late nights
And biting hounds

Angry games
Sister bosses
Unjust claims
And easy losses

Rainy days
Too much sun
Mean ways
And the end of fun

And may Jesus and Mary bring you safe to manhood
And help you remember with your own sons

What it was like to be a boy in summertime.
And God, the ever patient father of all of us
Bless you, Father, Son, and Holy Spirit.

A BLESSING FOR AN AUGUST WEDDING

May Jesus and Mary and Patrick be with you
And also Finbar and Finian and Fintnan
And Brendan and Colum and Brigid too
And Kathleen and Kevin and Killian*

May they sing you songs of hope and grace
And protect from all love-destroying harm
May they whisper stories of life and faith
And entice you to follow God's gentle charm

May you find in each other laughter and love
And courage in time of stress and strain
A hint of endless bliss in heaven above
And on earth the nerve to begin again

With fresh strawberries may you ever wait
When you seem to have wandered off the track
May the path ahead of you be wide and straight
And like they say the wind always at your back

And may the God who is love bless you
Father, Son and Holy Spirit

*Killian is the patron saint of Bavaria.

A BLESSING FOR HALLOWEEN

May the saints watch over you all the time
No matter where in the world you roam
May they protect you in every clime
And all of them bring you safely home

May their stories show God's tender care
And how good and kind you can really be
And that God waits for you just everywhere
With truth and hope that will make you free

And may the God of all the saints
Bless you, Father, Son and Holy Spirit

A BLESSING FOR NOVEMBER NIGHTS

As the days turn cold and
The winter nights grow long
May Brigid warm your hearts
And fill them with happy song

May Jesus and Mary
Grant you Thanksgiving cheer
Good Christmas shopping peace,
And love from those who are dear

For them may you be hope
And warmth and joy and light
At the end of each day
A hint of Christmas night

And may the God of laughter and love
Bless you, Father, Son, and Holy Spirit

A BLESSING FOR A PARTY

May Brigid, who wished for the pool of ale
Grant that the fun at the party will not fail
And may Jesus and Mary come to the party too
In the friendship and joy in each one of you

May you rejoice in all the good times past
And pray to God that such goodness always last
May you celebrate the richness of God's love for us
And clean up when all is done with only a little fuss

And may the God of celebrations bless all of you
Father, Son, and Holy Spirit.

A BLESSING FOR A HOUSE

May Jesus and Mary and Patrick be with this house
And all who come visit it,
Relative, friend, stranger,
May story and song and dance
Bring joy to all who live in it
And may love and friendship be stronger
Whenever they leave

May Jesus and the Holy Spirit
Always be present
Bringing with them
Faith and mystery and surprise
May all wicked feelings and nasty thoughts
Pass through these doors and be out again
As quickly as the wind blows off the Lake

May there always be food and drink
For the guest and for those who come in need.
May God protect this house
And all those who dwell in it
With the Love that He grants

To those who are part of Her family

And May of all us be part
Of God's family forever more.

Father, Son, and Holy Spirit

PRAYERS

A PRAYER FOR MIDSUMMER'S NIGHT

Oh God who loves us all more powerfully than any human lover, I thank you for the long days and the bright sunlight and the memories of festivities around this day. May the sunlight of your love brighten my life not only today but on all days of the year even when the sun has retreated from the sky and darkness closes in all around me. I ask this in the name of Jesus the Lord. Amen.

A PRAYER FOR THE BEGINNING
OF A SUMMER WEEKEND

Oh Lady Love, you are always with us in our work and our play. Stay close to us on this weekend. Keep the skies blue and the sun bright. Protect us from all danger and from impatience and ill temper. Help us to truly enjoy the blessings of this week, to relax, to laugh, to love. Send us back to our work on Monday better sons and daughters of you than we are today. We ask this in the name of Jesus your son. Amen.

A PRAYER FOR PRIESTS

Jesus, our high priest, you were human in all things save sin, so you understand the human frailties, fears, and weariness of our priests. Reassure and comfort them, illumine and challenge them. Give them hope and wisdom and grace so that they may lead all of us home to you. Help them to realize how important they are to the rest of us, now more important than ever; and send more young people into the priesthood to follow after you. Amen.

A PRAYER FOR THE ENVIRONMENT

Oh God, you reveal yourself in your creation, the earth and the air and the mountains and the waters and the forests and the fields and all the creatures therein. Help us to respect these sacraments of your presence and to use them for our needs with reverence and restraint. Grant that carelessness and greed may never again deface your creation. We ask this through Jesus your Son who took on human flesh and thus sanctified again all of creation. Amen.

A PRAYER FOR SIGHT

Creator of all the world and lover of each of us, help me to see the beauty with which you have surrounded me, the colors, the shades, the lights, the shadows, the shapes, the patterns, all the dazzling array of enchantments of the eye to which I usually pay so little attention. Help me to realize that I live in a many splendored land and to enjoy the splendors which you have given me as a hint of what you're really like. I ask this in the name of Jesus our savior. Amen.

A SUMMERTIME PRAYER

I thank you, Lady Wisdom, you who preside over the turning of the seasons and the long days and the short nights, for blessing me with summertime, with sunlight and heat, with sand and surf, with humid days and rainy nights. Grant that I may use well my summer respite for rest and recreation and recollection. Protect me and all those I love from summer dangers. Help us to see in the heat of summer a hint of the passion of your love. I ask this in the name of Jesus your Son. Amen.

A PRAYER IN GRATITUDE FOR PEACE

Thank you, Heavenly Father, for restoring peace. Bind up the wounds, heal the pain, cure the sick and wounded, send home the prisoners, purify the environment, remove the causes of future conflict, and protect us from the return of the horrors of war. We ask this in the name of your Son, the Prince of Peace. Amen.

A PRAYER AGAINST RESENTMENT

Lord Jesus who forgave those who tortured and murdered you help me to learn from your good example and to forgive my enemies, my false friends, those who turn against me because I have been generous to them, and my real friends who seem to use and exploit me. Purge resentment from my soul because with it I do more harm to myself than anyone else can do to me. I ask this of the Father in heaven in your name. Amen.

A PRAYER TO APPRECIATE
THE EUCHARIST

Lord Jesus who desired to be united with us in a community meal which is also a wedding banquet and who is present to us in the bread and wine we consume at this meal help me to comprehend with all my being the love that the Eucharist represents and offers and to share this comprehension with all around me. I ask this in your name of the Father and the Holy Spirit. Amen.

A PRAYER FOR COURAGE

God of power and might give me strength of conviction, depth of faith, and serene confidence in your love for me. Help me to believe that no matter what may happen or what others might do to me, your love is implacably faithful and no one can ever separate me from that love. I ask for this courage in the name of Jesus my Lord. Amen.

A PRAYER FOR PATIENCE

Lord God who is endlessly patient with my foolish and annoying frailties, instill in me patience for my fellow humans. Help me to keep my temper cool, my nerves calm, and my disposition amiable. Grant that noise and confusion and conflicts may not deprive me of the peace your Son came to bring to the word. I ask this in the name of the same Jesus our Lord. Amen.

A PRAYER WHEN DISCOURAGED

Jesus Lord who said that your yoke is sweet and your burden is light, lift up my weary soul, rekindle my enthusiasm, stimulate my energy, excite once again my imagination, and refresh my spirit. Do all these things for me, I beg you, so that I may serve you with greater generosity and deeper faith. I ask this of you together with the Father and the Spirit. Amen.

A PRAYER FOR TROUBLED FRIENDS

Lord God, who sent Jesus to bring peace and grace to all humankind, shower that grace on my troubled friends. May they find in your love illumination and reconciliation, hope and joy, and the resurrection experience of beginning again. Grant that they may understand that resurrection isn't supposed to be easy. I ask this in the name of the same Jesus. Amen.

A PRAYER FOR A RAINY DAY

Lady Love lift my spirits on this gloomy, rainy day. Let my good cheer be blue sky for those around me and let my smile be their sunlight. Let me radiate love that reflects your love and hints at the return of brightness tomorrow or, if it be your will, even this afternoon! Amen.

A PRAYER FOR LEADERS

Gracious Lord, who chose ordinary men in your twelve apostles, help those ordinary human beings who are my priests and bishops. Enlighten them, encourage them, give them vision and strength, purge them of pettiness and ambition that they may celebrate your love for everyone and lead the rest of us to you. We ask this through you of the Father and the Holy Spirit. Amen.

A PRAYER FOR UNDERSTANDING

Lord Jesus who through the writings of your apostle Paul told us that all we ever dreamed of, hoped for, and aspired to, has come true in you, grant that I may see how much your Father loves me and thus understand that in the end all manner of things will turn out well. I ask this through you of the Father and the Holy Spirit. Amen.

A PRAYER ON A MONDAY MORNING

Lady Love, the source of all life and goodness, on this morning of the first day of the week, fill me with enthusiasm and zeal for your work, stir up my ambition to serve you, renew my weakened hope and faith so that I might strive more vigorously for your kingdom in the day and week ahead. I ask for this rebirth in the name of your Son, Jesus the Lord. Amen.

A PRAYER FOR FAITH

Gracious creator of all that is, you whose love is revealed in both the galaxies and in the electrons and whose wisdom is disclosed to us in the marvelous designs of both immense and tiny realities, straighten my faith in your wisdom and your love, your power and your concern for me. Grant that I may realize that I live in a universe driven by passionate love and strive to return that love. I ask this through your Son, Jesus the Lord. Amen.

A PRAYER FOR FORGIVENESS

Oh God whose forgiving love was revealed in Hosea's pardon of his wife and Jesus's pardon of his murderers forgive me all the wrong I have done during by life whether because of weakness or inattention or passion or malice. Help me to rise again from the tomb of sin into the new life of your saving grace. I ask this through the same Jesus Our Lord. Amen.

A PRAYER IN TIME OF WORRY

O loving God without whose concern a single sparrow does not fall help me in my anxieties and concerns to know that in your power and love all manner of things will be well and that every tear dried, every hurt healed, every pain soothed. Grant that in times of worry I may manifest the confidence of the Spirit to all around me. I ask this in the name of the same Spirit and Jesus the Lord. Amen.

A PRAYER FOR MARRIED PEOPLE

Oh God whose passionate and tender love for us is revealed in the love between man and woman help my married friends whose love just now is troubled. Teach them patience and forgiveness, grant them faith in your protection and the courage to begin again. Renew in their hearts the love of their wedding day and direct them on the path of reconciliation if it be your will. I ask this in the name of Jesus the Lord. Amen.

A PRAYER WHEN TIRED

Jesus Lord, You know first hand the experience of human weariness and discouragement. Sustain me through this time when I am tired and depressed. Renew my vigor and enthusiasm that, refreshed and eager, I might work more diligently in spreading the good news you came to share with us. I ask this in your name, Jesus the Lord. Amen.

A PRAYER FOR THOSE FACING DEATH

Oh Lord who took on human flesh in the person of our Savior Jesus Christ so that you could walk the last mile to death with each of us, assist your servant who is now on that last mile. Give her courage and faith and especially hope that she may face death bravely and teach the rest of us how to die. Bring her home to you where her life will only just begin, and bring her home as gently as possible. We ask this in the name of Jesus the Lord. Amen.

A PRAYER DURING A VACATION

O Lord who has blessed me with this opportunity to relax and reflect, slow down the pace of my life and my activity and help me to use this precious and gifted time well so that I might better understand what you wish of me and return to my work in your service refreshed and renewed and with a clearer idea of the purposes of my life. I ask this in the name of Jesus the Lord. Amen.

A PRAYER
FOR PROTECTION AGAINST EVIL

Dear Lord who sent your Son Jesus into the world to overcome the power of evil protect me from the evil, human and not human, which lurks around me. Protect me with David under the shadow of your wings and with Patrick be my shield and my armor so that I may walk safely through life until it is time for my journey to end. I ask this in the name of the Jesus the Lord. Amen.

A PRAYER FOR THE CHURCH

Oh Lord whose body the Church is and who depends on the Church for the preaching of the Good News grant it leaders of courage and vision, of faith and integrity, of charm and dedication. Help them to lead us out of the swamp in which we are now mired so that we may move forward again in the service of the kingdom which you came to announce. I ask this in the name of Jesus the Lord. Amen.

A PRAYER TO SEEK
THE PEARL OF GREAT PRICE

Lady Wisdom, you who presided over the wonders of the universe in their construction and ordering, help me to find the most wonderful surprise of all, the pearl of truth and love which you have revealed through your Son Jesus and grant that I might dedicate myself to the life-long search for this precious jewel. I ask this in the name of the same Jesus Our Lord. Amen.

A PRAYER IN TIME OF FAILURE

Oh God who grants the increase for our labors help me to accept the inevitability of failure and my own personal failures. As you helped your Son Jesus rise up each time that he fell under the burden of his cross, give me strength to continue my work no matter how often I fail. I ask this in the name of Jesus the Lord. Amen.

A PRAYER THAT I MIGHT LOVE

Oh God who has told us so often that you are love, fill my heart with love for all I should love and who love me. Let not impatience or distraction or weariness interfere with love. Grant that I may try to be as generous in my love as you are in your love. Purify my love of selfishness and self-seeking and bind me and all I love with your own love. I ask this through Jesus who came to reveal your love to us. Amen.

A PRAYER FOR THE COMING OF GUESTS

Jesus Lord, you were a guest in many homes, treated more gently in some than in others, help us to see in our guests yourself come into our house and to treat our guests with the same respect and love with which we'd treat you.   Amen.

A PRAYER TO COOL IT

Lady Love, who takes care of each of us with a mother's attentive eye, help me to stay cool and confident in this busy time in my life. Protect me from frantic rush and hasty responses, from nervous nights and dismal days, from tightened gut and manic dashes. Grant that at all hours I may be the kind of child of which you will be proud. I ask this in the name of Jesus your son. Amen.

A PRAYER FOR THE SPIRIT

Spirit of Wisdom and Love, help me to hear your voice, feel your gentle winds, see your footprints, taste your sweetness, smell your perfume. Grant that I may always be open to your whisperings and ready to be inspired by the flames of your passionate love. I ask this of you and the Father and the Son. Amen.

A PRAYER IN FACE OF DEATH

Oh God who sent Jesus to promise us life grant that I may face death bravely and generously with the knowledge that my life, like all lives must end, and that death is not the end of life. Help me to understand that the only way to find my life is to be willing to lose it. I ask this in the name of the same Jesus the Lord. Amen.

A PRAYER FOR REALISM

Oh God on whom I depend for everything—the air I breath, the food I eat, the friends I love, my life itself—help me to understand that my existence is fragile, that my being hangs by a single thread, and that only your love sustains my existence. Grant that I may always understand how much I depend on you. I ask this in the name of Jesus the Lord. Amen.

A PRAYER FOR A DEPARTED FRIEND

Oh God who gives us such great dreams and so short a life, grant peace and rest to my departed friend. May he find in you all that his dreams ever imagined and more. May the emptiness in my life be filled by faith and may I learn from his death how fleeting is life and how powerful is your love. I ask this in the name of Jesus my Lord. Amen.

A PRAYER FOR THE BEREAVED

Lady Wisdom, who with a mother's love wipes away our tears and makes all manner of things well, look with tenderness and affection on those who suffer pain and loss. Heal their grief, straighten their faith, help them to understand that all separations, however traumatic, are only temporary and that together with you we will all be young again and all laugh again. I ask this through Jesus your son. Amen.

A PRAYER FOR THOSE WHO WORK

Oh Lord who worked as a carpenter and the son of a carpenter bless and protect all those who work for a living. Grant that they be paid just wages and be protected from abuse and corruption. Grant also that those all over the world who work hard may be blessed with the same rewards for their labor as those with which we Americans are blessed. We ask these blessings of the Father in your name. Amen.

A PRAYER FOR LOVE

Oh God who is love, help me to understand my total dependence on your love. Help me to respond to that love with love of my own. Help me to love others as You love them and as you love me. Help me to see in those who love me the most, hints of you and your love. Help me to realize that my life makes sense only when I realize that I am adrift in a sea of love. I ask this in the name of Jesus the Lord. Amen.

A PRAYER ON A GRAY DAY

Oh God who charms us by the changing of the days and the seasons lift up my spirits on this seemingly spiritless day. Grant that my joy over your love for me may break through the clouds and the darkness and be sunlight for all those around me. I ask this in the name of Jesus the Lord. Amen.

A PRAYER TO THE HOLY SPIRIT

Come, O Dancing God, O Spirit of Life and Love, of Beauty and Variety and Diversity, stir up my somber soul, bathe me in your light, lead me by your fire, unleash my own leaden spirit that I may dance with you and be light for those around me and reflect your love to all that I love. I ask this in the name of Jesus the Lord. Amen.

A PRAYER FOR UNDERSTANDING

Jesus, light of the world, help me to understand as best I can in this time of confusion and uncertainty, of mystery and bafflement, what is the purpose of my life, how I should respond to its problems, and the presence of your Father's love in all the tragedies and glories of the human condition. Grant that I may see a little more clearly. Amen.

A PRAYER FOR PROTECTION

O gracious God who has given us life and health, protect us against human wickedness, against the envious and the malicious, the ambitious and the demented, the sick and the crazy, against those who hate us and would destroy us. May we resist them with charity and patience, but protect those we love against them nonetheless. And do you, guardian of our homes and our love, keep them away from our door. We ask for this protection in the name of Jesus the Lord. Amen.

A PRAYER AGAINST ENVY

O Lord God whose Son Jesus was falsely accused by the envious, protect me from those who envy me and would destroy me if they could and protect me from feeling envy towards those whose talent and success threatens me. Grant that I may rejoice always in your goodness and generosity, no matter who is the recipient. Help me to be as generous as you are in all my thoughts, words, and deeds. Amen.

A PRAYER IN MELANCHOLY

Oh gracious Lord who created us to be happy in your service, lift the clouds from my spirit that I may bask in the rays of your saving sunlight. Come to my melancholy soul and set it on fire with love and joy so that I might better serve you in whatever days I have left in my life. I ask this in the name of Jesus the Lord. Amen.

A PRAYER FOR FORGIVENESS

Oh God, you who are the personification of forgiveness, you whom Jesus depicted as the indulgent farmer, the father of the prodigal son, the good Samaritan, forgive me all that I have done wrong in life and help me to understand that your eagerness to forgive me is greater by far than my need to be forgiven. Grant that I may believe that in your love, I am already forgiven. I ask this in the name of the same Jesus your Son. Amen.

A PRAYER FOR RESIGNATION

Lord Jesus, who died so horribly on the cross, help me to be resigned to my own death with whatever sufferings and terrors it might bring. Do not let my fear of death paralyze my life. Grant that I may die as I try to live -- in the warm embrace of God's love. Most of all strengthen my faith that life and love are stronger than death. Amen.

A PRAYER
ON THE LAST SUNDAY IN OCTOBER

Oh God who brings us both light and darkness, I mourn the lost of light and accept the coming of darkness. Grant that as darkness grows stronger and light weaker in the days and weeks to come, my faith in your triumph over sin and death may be as certain as the eventual return of light. I ask this in the name of Jesus, the light of the world. Amen.

A PRAYER AT THE END OF AN ILLNESS

Oh Lady Love, thank you for beginning the restoration of my health. Grant that I may learn from this sickness the fragility of my human organism and my total dependence on you. May my recovery be complete so that I may serve you with renewed enthusiasm. Finally I pray that I may learn from my illness how hard it is to pray when I am sick and that therefore I may work ever more diligently on my habits of prayer. I ask this of Jesus your Son who came at Christmas time to heal the whole world. Amen.

A PRAYER FOR PATIENCE

Gracious Lord, You who created everything in a Big Bang and yet let the process go on for billions of years, teach me to practice the balance between patience and enthusiasm. Grant that I may never become lethargic and that I also may not too often be impulsive and compulsive in my own work. Help me to understand the rhythms of the days and the seasons of my own life and to make those rhythms the paradigms for my work. I ask this in the name of Jesus our patient Lord. Amen.

A PRAYER FOR PROTECTION

O great angels of heaven, so often ignored now by us but remembered and honored by others, messengers of God and protectors of humans, stretch forth your power and might, protect us from war and sickness and injustice and accident and, as I used to pray, may one of you always be at my side to light, to guard, to rule, to guide. Amen.

A PRAYER FOR COMPLETE RECOVERY

O Loving Jesus who came to heal those who were sick both spiritually and physically, please restore my health to its fullness, exorcise the remaining germs, help my body to regain its resistance and strength, do all these things please so that I might better serve you. Amen.

A PRAYER FOR DEPARTED FRIENDS

Oh God of mercy and peace, I miss my friends who are no longer with us. Grant them light and rest in the home towards which we all journey. Give me the courage and faith to follow them on the road of this life and the bravery I will need when I cross the boundary and join them on the way home. I ask this in the name of Jesus my Lord. Amen.

A PRAYER FOR UNDERSTANDING

Oh God who made me absolutely unique help me to value more the person you made me to be. Protect me from comparisons and envy and discouragement over what I am not. Inspire me to become more the person that I am and that I should be. Grant that I may understand that you love me, faults and all, and that I may accept myself even as you accept me. I ask this in the name of Jesus the Lord. Amen.

A PRAYER OF THANKSGIVING

O God from whom all blessings come we thank you for this house and the dunes and the lake around it. We also thank you for all the joy with which you have blessed us in the last twenty five years. May our lives shine forth as bright lights of gratitude for all your gifts so that the world may know of your love for humankind. We ask this in the name of Jesus the Lord. Amen.

A PRAYER FOR ADVENT

Jesus, my Lord, as you brought light into the darkness of an old and weary world, light and youth and energy, guide me through this dark and dreary time of the year and bring me to the joys of Christmas and the promise of spring to come with a heart filled with laughter and love. I ask this of the Father in your name. Amen.

A PRAYER FOR CHRISTMAS EVE

Lady Love, whose maternal affection for us is revealed in Mary the Mother of Jesus, bring us with the shepherds to Bethlehem so that we can see in the image of the Madonna and Child the passionate gentleness of your affection for us and in that image gain strength and hope for all our lives. We ask this in the name of the Babe born at Bethlehem and his mother. Amen.

A PRAYER FOR CHRISTMAS DAY

Heavenly Father, Gracious Mother, who have sent Jesus into the world to seal your love affair with humankind, grant that in the family joy of this Christmas festival we may welcome you into our families and with your presence transform our family life so that it will mirror your love for us. We ask this in the name of Jesus the Lord. Amen.

A PRAYER FOR NEW YEAR'S DAY

Mary, Mother of all of us, on this festival in your honor at Christmas time, win for us the graces we need to be good and loyal children during the coming year, even as you offer to himself our gratitude for all the many blessings with which he has enriched our lives during the year that has just ended. We ask this in the name of the same Jesus Our Lord. Amen.

A PRAYER FOR THE EPIPHANY

Gracious Lord, you who revealed God's affection for us to the Wise Men, at the Transfiguration, and at Cana and Galilee, help us to realize that our vocation, like yours, is to let God's light shine among our fellow humans by kindness, generosity, dedication and love. We ask for these gifts in your name. Amen.

A PRAYER AGAINST WAR

Prince of Peace, you who came into the world to bring the peace that the world cannot give, consider all those lives which will be snuffed out, all those who will grieve for their losses, and grant that there be no war. Enlighten the minds and move the hearts of leaders on both sides and grant that the conflict may be peacefully resolved. We ask this of the Father in Heaven, who loves all equally, in your name. Amen.

A PRAYER FOR GENEROSITY

O God who created galaxies and worlds without number, animals and plants, and microbes beyond count, and tiny subatomic particles we can barely imagine, help us to be as bountiful and gracious to those we love as you have been to us. Grant that we do not fall victim to the temptation of converting your generous word to an ideology which gives us power over others. We ask all of these things in the name of Jesus your son and Our Lord. Amen.

A PRAYER FOR PEACE

Take pity, Gracious Lord, on the mothers and the wives and the sweethearts and the daughters and the sons and fathers and brothers and husbands of those who are in combat during these terrible days. Spare them, if you can, from lives of pain and grief and bring the ones they love home safely. We ask this in the name of Jesus the Lord. Amen.

A PRAYER FOR THE CHILDREN

Good Lord, children are dying in this terrible war, innocent children who have done nothing to anyone. We Americans are not killing them deliberately, but we are killing them just the same -- and with little grief or guilt. Protect those who are still alive, cure their wounds and their horror, and give them hope for the life ahead of them. Bring home to your love those who have already died and grant that there be no more deaths. We ask this in the name of Jesus the Lord. Amen.

A PRAYER OF GRATITUDE

I wish to offer thanks, O God of justice and mercy, that so few Americans died in the war and I wish also to beg you to touch the hardened hearts of my fellow Americans so they will feel grief and compassion, if not some sense of guilt, for all the Iraqi soldiers and civilians who did die. Forgive our crimes against innocent people and grant that in the flush of victory (for what was probably a just cause) we may not lose sight of the terrible suffering this war caused to others. I ask this in the name of Jesus your Son and of Mary his mother. Amen.

A PRAYER FOR SAINT PATRICK'S DAY

Good Saint Patrick, you are alleged (with reason, doubtless) to have expelled the snakes from Ireland. Expel also the snakes from the hearts of Irish Americans on this day -- the snakes of arrogance and pride, of contentiousness and drunkenness, of boisterousness and bigotry. Ask herself to grant that they may realize that the true spirit of your adopted country is gentleness and wit, loyalty and generosity, patience and charm. I address this large order to you in the name of Jesus the Lord and Mary his mother. Amen.

A PRAYER TO SAINT BRIGID

O Saint of spring and poetry and new life, bring the gift of poetry and the life of spring to my dull and weary soul. Stir up in me again the Irish gift of laughter and hope and let me once again sing your praises -- and hers too. Mary of the Gaels, bring this request to herself for me in the name of Jesus Our Lord, who you are said to have nursed. Amen.

A PRAYER FOR THREE IRISH TEENAGERS*

Bless with eternal happiness, gentle Lady, these three young people, shot at a candy stand by a masked gunman. Grant that the sweetness of their candy proves a hint of the sweetness of the home they now share with you. Console their families for the loss of three young lives and bring peace to the troubled land where they lived so that no more young lives with be destroyed by fanatics with guns.   Amen.

*Two young women working at an outdoor candy stand and a young customer were gunned down by a masked gunman in Northern Ireland. A Protestant "militant" group claimed credit for the killing.

A PRAYER FOR ST. VALENTINE

Saint of romantic lovers, outcast from the Roman calendar, ask that God stir up today romantic passion for all who look to you as their patron. May they see in their enthrallment of one another a hint of God's ardent love for all of us. And may they learn from the renewal of romance that it is always possible to begin again. Finally, may the Church realize how important you are and restore you to the calendar. Amen.

A PRAYER FOR ASH WEDNESDAY

O God who called us forth from dust and breathed into us the soul of life and a hunger for immortality and for you, help us to remember that not only are we made from dust and will return to dust but that we are also destined to rise again and live forever in glory with you. Increase our hope and faith so that we will always remember that death does not have the final word over life. We ask this in the name of the Risen Jesus. Amen.

A PRAYER IN THE MIDDLE OF LENT

Lady Love, Lent goes by too quickly as does my life. Help me to take advantage of all the opportunities you give me. Don't let me be so caught up in the demands of the day – the phone, the doorbell, the deadline – that I lose touch with you and the invitation to love which you always offer me. I ask this in the name of Jesus the Lord. Amen.

A PRAYER FOR PALM SUNDAY

On this Sunday, Lord Jesus, when we celebrate in anticipation your triumph over sin and death, help us to realize that the story, the drama, the excitement of this week all exist to show us how much God loves us and the extent to which He will go to unite himself to the human condition. In this knowledge grant that we may rejoice because all things will finally end well. We ask this in the name of the same Jesus our Lord. Amen.

A PRAYER FOR PRIESTS
ON HOLY THURSDAY

Jesus Lord, who chose your priests from among humans so that they might understand the nature of human weakness, confirm your priests today in their vocations. Grant that they may know that they are the light of the world, the salt of the earth, the dessert after dinner, the leaders of your people. And grant, too, that there will be others to follow after them in your service. Amen.

A PRAYER ON GOOD FRIDAY

Help me to understand, Jesus my Savior, that the theme today is not suffering but triumph over suffering, that you won a victory for all of us by showing us how to die, and that, after your death, no suffering is ever without purpose and that no one ever dies in vain. Grant that through your example I will learn how to live and how to die. Amen.

A PRAYER ON HOLY SATURDAY

Oh God of fire and water, of male and female, of renewal and life, of happy faults and new beginnings, of passionate union and bright new birth, stir up in our hearts the memory of all of the new beginnings in our life so that we may link them with the glory of the Resurrection of Jesus and the rebirth in baptism which we celebrate tonight. We ask this blessing through the Risen Jesus. Amen.

A PRAYER FOR EASTER SUNDAY

Oh God who bestows life prodigious and of whose abundant graciousness the rabbit and the egg and the lily are symbols, renew our life of faith on this morning of joy and help us to sing the alleluia with confidence and hope that some day, just like Jesus, we too will rise again. We ask this in the name of the Risen Jesus. Amen.

A PRAYER ON THOMAS SUNDAY

O God on whose grace even the smallest amount of faith totally depends help us to believe in the Resurrection of Jesus as a sign of your love and a promise of the triumph of our own lives over death. Strengthen, deepen, and enrich our faith so that the joy and confidence of our lives may help bring the Good News of your love to the ends of the earth. Amen.

A PRAYER FOR A PRIEST

Lord Jesus, this man has served you well in the priesthood for forty years, he has indeed been a light to the nations and a source of comfort and challenge to his people. He has indeed revealed to them the depth of your commitment and of the Heavenly Father's commitment to them. Bless him and protect him in the years to come and help him to always be the kind of priest he is today, only even better. Amen.

A PRAYER FOR IRELAND

Yet again, Lady Wisdom, they have come together to try to find the path of peace in this land of terrible beauty. Help them all, on both sides, to be open and sensitive to one another, to understand that hatred and murder in your Son's name is the worst of blasphemies and that if they truly are his followers they will strive to find ways of peace and justice. Grant that the killing may finally stop and that the healing might at last begin. We ask for this peace in the name of Jesus your Son. Amen.

A PRAYER FOR THE INAUGURATION
OF A MAYOR

Oh Lord, who blesses us with leaders to help us find our way through the mysteries and turmoils of life, guide and protect our new mayor. Help him to lead us with confidence and integrity, wisdom and courage, patience and wit, laughter and love. May he be an example to the city of generosity and responsibility and of sympathy and kindness. Grant that he and his family may always have the humor to survive the difficult times and humility to survive the good times. We ask for all these blessings -- and any more you can think of -- in the name of Jesus the Lord. Amen.

A PRAYER FOR ASCENSION THURSDAY

Come back, Lord Jesus, even as You went away and were hidden by a cloud. Return out of the cloud and finish the work you started. Remain with us always so that we will know You in the breaking of the bread. Grant us energy when we are tired, vision when we are blind, courage when we are afraid, wisdom when we are confused, and love when we are angry. Never leave us again. We ask this, God in heaven, in Jesus' name. Amen.

A PRAYER FOR PENTECOST

O Holy Spirit, spinning, whirling, dancing God of variety and diversity, help us to rejoice in all your wondrous works. Grant that we may celebrate both the uniqueness of each of us as an individual person and the buzzing blooming variety of the world in which you are the Spirit of "Here Comes Everyone." May there be room in the community of those who follow You not only for Parthians and Medes and Elamites but also for New Yorkers and Californians and Texans. Come dance with all of us, O Dancing God. Amen.

A PRAYER FOR APRIL

Lady Love, we give you all credit for this glorious April sunshine which has brought spring greenery to Chicago a month early. Even though we know it won't last, we still pray that you will help us to see the bursting out of spring as a revelation of your generous and fertile mother love. Grant that our bodies and souls be filled with the warmth of that love. We ask this in the name of your Son, Jesus the Lord. Amen.

A PRAYER FOR MARY'S MONTH

Mother Mary, during this the fairest month of all the year, may we always remember that you reveal to us the mother love of God and that the image of Madonna and child is also an image of God and us. Help us to see that God loves each of us with a mother's passion, even greater than the one you experienced when you held Jesus in your arms. And, should St. Peter lock us out of the front door of heaven, please be on guard at the back door so that we may be safe with you, as the Irish say, a half-hour before the devil knows we're dead. Amen.

A MEMORIAL DAY PRAYER

Help us to remember on this day, Lord, the bravery of the men who fought and died to protect our country. Grant that our memory of their sacrifices may spur us to avoid as best we can future wars which may call on other young men and women to make similar sacrifices. May we come to see that the costs of war are enormous and that it should be avoided whenever possible. We beg this in the name of Jesus the Lord. Amen.

A PRAYER FOR SUMMERTIME

We thank you, Gracious Lord, for sending summer and its pleasures -- for beaches and patio parties, for sailing and swimming and water skiing and baseball and softball and for vacations with family and friends. Help us to understand that these summer joys are but a hint of what you have prepared for those who respond to your Love. Grant that we may never forget you in the midst of our summer fun. Amen.

A PRAYER ON THE FOURTH OF JULY

Lord Jesus, you came into the world that we might all be free of sin and death. We Americans believe that political freedom is a secular reflection of that basic freedom. We thank you and through you the Father in heaven for our political freedom. Help us never to take it for granted and to strive that freedom be experienced by everyone in our land, especially the poor and the oppressed, and eventually by all of humankind. Amen.

A LABOR DAY PRAYER

Lord Jesus, you who were known as a carpenter and the son of a carpenter, look with favor on all those who work for a living. Bless them with pride in their work, a just wage for their efforts, and safety in the places where they work. Grant that all exploitation of working men and women be banished from the face of the earth and especially from within our Church. We ask these gifts of the Father in your name.   Amen.

A PRAYER IN THE MORNING

O God, for whose fidelity to us the rising sun is a promise, protect and guide me through this day. Help me in the distractions and the frustrations, the disillusion and the disappointment, the failure and the pain. Help me too in the joy and the love, the successes and the rewards, the fun and the laughter. I offer all these events, good and bad, to you in the name of Jesus the Lord. Amen.

A PRAYER AT NIGHT

Lady Wisdom, thank you for the many graces of this day, one less day in my life. I am sorry for my many failures today and grateful for your many blessings. As I collapse into sleep let me remember with my last waking thought that you love me, always have and always will; and, after a peaceful sleep, let me rise again in your service and in anticipation of the final rising when your son returns. I offer this night prayer in his name. Amen.